CANCER

CANCER

Let your Sun sign show you the way
to a happy and fulfilling life

Marion Williamson & Pam Carruthers

SIRIUS

SIRIUS

This edition published in 2022 by Sirius Publishing, a division of
Arcturus Publishing Limited,
26/27 Bickels Yard, 151–153 Bermondsey Street,
London SE1 3HA

Copyright © Arcturus Holdings Limited

All rights reserved. No part of this publication may be reproduced, stored in a retrieval system, or transmitted, in any form or by any means, electronic, mechanical, photocopying, recording or otherwise, without written permission in accordance with the provisions of the Copyright Act 1956 (as amended). Any person or persons who do any unauthorised act in relation to this publication may be liable to criminal prosecution and civil claims for damages.

ISBN: 978-1-3988-0857-7
AD008748UK

Printed in China

CONTENTS

Introduction

*W*elcome, Cancer! You have just taken a step towards what might become a lifelong passion. When astrology gets under your skin, there's no going back. Astrology helps you understand yourself and the people around you, and its dazzling insights become more fascinating the deeper you go.

Just as the first humans turned to the life-giving Sun for sustenance and guidance, your astrological journey begins with your Sun sign of Cancer. First, we delve deeply into the heart of what makes you tick, then we'll continue to unlock your cosmic potential by exploring love, your career and health, where you might prefer to live, and how you get along with family and friends.

Then it's over to gifted astrologer, Pam Carruthers, for her phenomenal birthdate analysis, where she gives personality insights for your specific Cancer birthday.

In the last part of the book we get right inside how astrology works by revealing the different layers that will help you understand your own birth chart and offer the planetary tools to get you started.

Are you ready, Cancer? Let's take a look underneath that tough shell of yours to see what's inside …

CUSP DATES FOR CANCER
22 June – 22 July

The exact time of the Sun's entry into each zodiac sign varies every year, so it's impossible to list them all. If you were born a day either side of the dates above, you're a 'cusp' baby. This means you may feel like you're a blend of Cancer/Gemini or Cancer/Leo or you may instinctively just know that you're one sign right to your core.

Going deeper

If you want to know once and for all whether you're a Gemini, Cancer or Leo, you can look up your birth date in a planetary ephemeris, of which there are plenty online. (See page 102 for more information). This shows the exact moment the Sun moved into a new zodiac sign for the month you were born.

The Cancer personality

uled by the Moon, your ever-changing moods reflect the lunar cycles as they wax and wane. In astrology the Moon represents our emotions, instincts and reactions, and with your Sun in the Moon's territory, your feelings are magnified. The Crab is your zodiac symbol, depicting your tough, outer personality – protecting and hiding the softer, more vulnerable, inner you.

You appear well-organised and quietly confident, like the captain of a ship in charge of everyone on board. You don't need, or want, to be the centre of attention. You know what you're doing, and you're a private person who just wants to be left alone to get on with things. Your kindly, firm, maternal manner, garners trust from the people around you who instinctively understand that you're looking out for them and are happy for you to take control.

You can be a little shy, and even standoffish, with people you don't know, but that's just because you're such a giving person. People need to earn your trust before you reveal what a sensitive soul you are inside. It would drain your mental and emotional energy to invite just anyone under your shell. Over the years the people closest to you appreciate that you take your time to break new ground and they give you a bit more time and space to get used to new people and situations.

Your confidence in people has probably been hard won. From an early age you may have been criticised for being too over-sensitive, too touchy or over-reactive and been told you need to 'toughen up' or 'live in the real world'. As a result, you built a shell, a protective wall around your heart, which works pretty well as a defence from an uncaring and unpredictable world. Like a lighthouse in a storm, you stand firm and strong in the toughest conditions. Your emotional states may be in an eternal state of fluctuation and agitation, but your values, desires and ambitions remain unchanged.

TENACIOUS AND DEFENSIVE

When you set your heart or mind on something, you're impressively tenacious. You're not usually impulsive or forthright, preferring to wait and watch before deciding on a course of action. Like a crab under the cover of moonlight, you're too self-conscious to strut your stuff and launch yourself into the middle of the action. When you have your eyes on the prize, you're clever and focussed, but rarely approach your goals directly.

A sidling, undercover advance, keeps you hidden from danger, and then at the last moment, when the coast is clear, you'll raise your pincers, grab your treasure then scuttle back to the safety of your home.

Once in your possession, you guard your treasures fiercely. The things that a true Cancer values most in life are home, family, food, money, old friends, memories and sentimental objects. You're not a feisty person generally but threaten the things you care about and you'll get very defensive – even a little aggressive – in your desires to keep hold of the things that matter.

LETTING GO

Partly because you find it so hard to let go, you have an affinity with old things – and that includes the past. You tend to romanticise or hark back to a better time, probably because it feels safer to lose yourself in memories, than to deal with an uncertain future. A lover of tradition, antiques and history, you attach sentimental value to things that baffle your nearest and dearest: old photographs, ugly or cumbersome items given to you by people long departed, or perhaps an attic stuffed with old baby clothes and toys. You still find comfort in these old things and guard them carefully. Ancient love letters, records and even bus tickets that remind you of a special person or period in your life – they all remind you of a time you felt loved and safe. In extreme cases, you no longer see these things as clutter but, often quite unconsciously, as more of an extension of your own protective layer or shell.

One of your greatest life lessons is to let go of past hurts. This is particularly hard for you to do because your memory is so incredibly good. You, more than any other sign, have detailed memories from childhood of people, pets and events that others have long forgotten.

But clinging to old ideas of yourself, or not forgiving people who let go of you, stop you from evolving and venturing forward into the world ... but the world really needs you!

CARING AND CATASTROPHIZING

Whether you're male or female, the Moon is linked with motherhood and you are a born caregiver. Your instincts are to love, nurture and protect without asking for much in return. You're a tough nut to crack because inside you're the softest, most beautiful soul, sensitive and easily hurt. Once you care, and let people into your enormous heart, you don't quite know how to give them up.

You're the zodiac's most impressive worrier. Because you have such an impressive memory, you can recall in detail when things went wrong in the past. Most people eventually move on with hazy memories of past failures – not you. You vowed to yourself that you'd never get into that kind of pain again, and to avoid it in future you promised never to forget. This mistrust of the world causes you anxiety and can rob you of the confidence you need to venture out your shell again. You are super-sensitive to your environment and your ever-changing moods and pessimism are just how you cope with life's unpredictability and harshness.

You love nothing better than a bit of catastrophizing because it confirms your fears that everything is about to go terribly wrong. You're the person that brings up that one time when things *did* go badly in the past – and your memory of it is crystal clear – even if you weren't actually there! You're no stranger to a bit of overdramatising for effect and feel it's your duty to help other people prepare for inevitable calamities.

When things do go awry for people you love, you're genuinely sympathetic. Their pain and disappointment chimes with your own vulnerabilities, and you're a wonderful listener. Never judgmental or harsh, you don't question much about what happened – someone you love is in trouble, that's enough. You'll offer the coat off your back, a warm, safe place to spend a few nights, and a nourishing meal. It won't even enter your mind that you may be inconvenienced or put you out of pocket for a while. The people you love come first, end of story.

LAUGHING UNTIL YOU CRY

All Cancer people are capable of a little lunar madness and, especially when younger, you'll be a slave to your constantly wavering inner landscape. Absorbing the moods of others, you know how they're feeling, perhaps even before they do.

You will no doubt have learned that other people don't always mean to hurt you with their thoughtless comments or insensitive actions.

Most people are nowhere near as tuned into the world of feeling as you, and would be mortified to think you'd taken offence. They're genuinely confused by your hurt reactions, baffled you could take such a trivial thing to heart. If you're really hurt by someone's behaviour you retreat into your shell, the silent treatment usually gets your message across. But if a loved one has angered you, it's a different story. It happens rarely, but when you take revenge it's usually in secret, quietly executed, and devastating!

Thank goodness you have an excellent sense of humour to take the sting out of the most emotionally tense situations. Laughing reminds you that nothing is ever that bad – even if it feels really intense. You love it when beloved friends have the nerve to poke fun at you – because you know there is no malice intended.

CAPRICORN LESSON

Your opposite sign of the zodiac reflects certain areas of your personality that you have not explored or fully developed. Usually you share many similarities but it's where they differ that compels the opposite signs together. Where Cancer is the sign of retreat and the private domain of home and family, Capricorn teaches you that if you trust, and take things slowly, you have something very valuable to offer the world at large. Capricorn is ambitious but steady and they usually work their way to the top of their chosen career. The Goat shows you how to make your mark in the business world, and that you can show a different side of yourself in your professional life. As long as you have a safe home base to return to, and learn to keep healthy boundaries between work and family, you will quickly replace stressful memories with good experiences. And when that happens you discover that you're actually a born leader!

Cancer
Motto

FAMILY IS NOT
AN IMPORTANT
THING.
IT'S EVERYTHING.

Cancer in love

*W*hen you're attracted to someone it scares you a little. Your first instinct is to hide and think it through, which usually means worrying about how things could pan out. After all, it could all go miserably wrong … like that time you were hurt in the past … or when your friend's husband was caught cheating. Your mind spins out before you know any real facts about your sexy stranger.

Training your imagination will probably turn out to be a lifetime's endeavour and you have such a tender heart that romance may be something of a learning process. As you get older and better understand your own and others' requirements in relationships, you'll learn to be more realistic. But you, more than any other zodiac sign, have the emotional capacity and understanding to navigate the human heart.

GIVING YOURSELF AWAY

When someone intriguing takes the first steps to get to know you, it can set off your defence mechanisms, and you'll be wary. Secretly you'll be flattered, but you'll worry yourself into a frenzy. And all this happens before you even know if this person is even truly flirting with you. You understand what a big deal giving even a tiny piece of your heart is – because the rest of your heart is usually close behind.

When you've been reassured enough from a potential lover, or have decided to trust him or her anyway, you are one of the most romantic people in the zodiac. You're an imaginative and generous lover and you'll place your partner at the centre of your universe.

COME INSIDE MY SHELL

When you choose to love somebody, you're all-in. When you let someone inside that crabby shell, there's no half measures. Domestic bliss is your aim and setting up a home and family will be paramount. Whether you're angling for a big house full of children or are happy with a pretty little garden and a budgie, your home set-up is where you feel safe, secure and loved.

You put down roots when you're at home, intending to build a base for life and your partner needs to share that vision. Fire and Air signs may be too independent and adventurous for you to settle down with, or you'll need to make sure you both have a clear understanding of what the other needs. As long as the trust is there, you can be happy with someone who wants space to do their own thing.

Emotional compatibility is the single most important factor in your relationships. Your bond with a lover is so tight that you'll feel it if something isn't right – and will be hurt or confused if they're not sharing every emotion with you. You expect to be able to talk to your other half about everything – and expect the same level of openness from him or her. You make it so easy for others to express themselves that this isn't usually a problem. And when you have a contented, established relationship with a happy home life, you'll love without asking for much in return.

TRICKY EMOTIONS

When your emotional needs are met, you tend to place your partner on a pedestal. You will defend their actions, and sometimes excuse them, even when friends or family might raise an eyebrow. It can take a lot of talking you around to see that your loved ones are anything but perfect.

When you do have a disagreement with your partner things can get heated fast and the insecurity can knock you off balance. Your fight or flight response is strong, and disagreements or misunderstandings can fill you with foreboding. Your beloved may accuse you of being overly dramatic or too needy, and that can wound you. It's difficult for you to remember that all relationships have to navigate a few hurdles from time to time, without causing insurmountable problems.

Even when there's nothing to worry about, your oversensitive nervous system may pick up on others' energies and you'll be tempted to interpret them to suit your own suspicions. This can leave your partner feeling bewildered and perplexed. It may take a while for your defences to come down again but, when they do, you'll be back to being one of the most generous and loving souls in the zodiac.

Most compatible love signs

Taurus – you both crave security, loyalty and a healthy bank balance and you'll adore each other's sensual nature, too.

Capricorn – your opposite sign is patient and reassuring and can teach you how to balance home and career.

Scorpio – you understand Scorpios because you are both emotionally driven with cool exteriors – they'll be tolerant of your changeable moods.

Least compatible love signs

Aquarius – you want someone to build a comfortable home with, but Aquarius has plans to join the circus.

Sagittarius – warm-hearted, enthusiastic but tactless, you need someone to be your soulmate, not your puppy.

Libra – they say all the right things, but do they *feel* them?

Cancer at work

Your ideal work situation involves looking after people to some degree. One-to-one employment on a personal basis such as a healthcare professional, counsellor or beauty therapist fulfils your selfless enjoyment of making other people happy. But your understated, excellent people skills also mean you would excel as a charity CEO, a public relations consultant, or as a politician campaigning for better conditions in your community.

You also love working with food – it's your way of nurturing people and it's not by accident you're known as the best cook in the zodiac. Working as a chef or in the catering industry would suit you well with your caretaking, comforting abilities. While in an office you often assume the role of the mother or father figure, lending a sympathetic ear, making sure everyone is happy, comfortable and listened to.

You're that popular work-mum who spoils your colleagues with fabulous homemade cakes or assumes the protective father figure – the union rep or person who sits on the staff counsel.

Your discretion and good judgment will be an asset whether you are an office manager or a HR director. And your commitment to solving problems, and attention to detail, ensure that you'd be an impressive project manager.

Wherever you work with other people your instincts are to protect and encourage them, whether they're children, elderly people or plants! Cancer is as green-fingered as Taurus when it comes to gardening. Working as a farmer, professional gardener or brewer, would also satisfy your instinct to nurture, cultivate and nourish.

HOME SECURITY

Like Taurus, you prefer a regular salary. You're better with money than most, appreciating its security. You're a saver at heart and even when you're pretty flush by anyone else's standards you're likely to plead poverty. The thought of not being able to pay your rent or mortgage, or risking your home, is one of your biggest anxieties and you're not frightened of taking on jobs that others would turn their noses up at to keep a roof over your head.

If you're in charge of putting food on the table at home, you'll clean streets, unblock toilets or busk outside the train station in the pouring rain if it brings in enough cash to care for your children. It's this dedication to others that also causes you to be a passionate fundraiser or advocate for people less fortunate than yourself.

If you're looking for work, you'll usually find it. In your quietly tenacious way, you'll prove yourself invaluable. You're stealthily ambitious and determined to keep your position for as long as possible. Your people-handling skills and unassuming manner impresses most employers who will appreciate your loyalty and calm, collected manner.

Freelance work or self-employment is fine, as long as you're watching your bank balance rise steadily. But if the cashflow runs low, or you're living on credit cards, you'll be an unhappy Crab!

CRABBY BOSS

Behind your shy exterior beats the heart of a leader! As a gentle, but firm, parental figure, you often rise to the top of your profession. Co-workers admire your quiet, strong leadership skills and learn that a little cajoling and kindness from you is sometimes all that's needed to exert authority. You're not a demanding or aggressive boss, preferring to connect with your work buddies on a more personal level.

Your colleagues feel comfortable with you and appreciate that you're sympathetic to their family needs. You'll pick up any vibes if things are off-kilter and understand what's needed to resolve any conflict. You care, but you will also demand loyalty.

If an employee, or a member of your team, decides to leave, you can't help but take it a little personally. It can feel like someone in your family is rebelling against you or has outgrown the nest. When workplace relationships feel strained you worry. And a stressed-out Crab will go inside their shell if they feel they're being attacked – even if that's just in their imagination!

Most compatible colleagues

Cancer – kindred spirits, you both appreciate how to make and save money and you're both very tactful around each other.

Virgo – you both enjoy helping others and Virgo responds well to your humble leadership style.

Pisces – Pisces likes peace and privacy in their working environment and you both appreciate that not everyone has to shout about their accomplishments.

Least compatible colleagues

Leo – you're good at spotting money-making opportunities and Leo's good at spending it!

Libra – isn't as ambitious as you and sees work as an extension of their social life.

Gemini – great at multitasking – not so good at concentrating on important details.

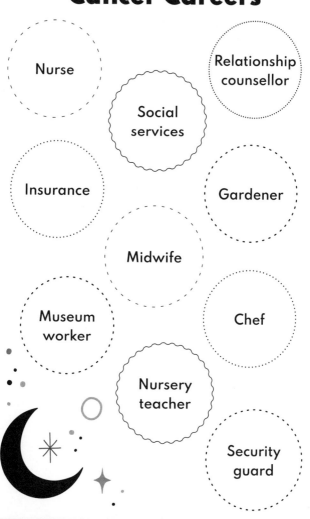

Perfect
Cancer Careers

Nurse

Relationship counsellor

Social services

Insurance

Gardener

Midwife

Museum worker

Chef

Nursery teacher

Security guard

Cancer
Work Motto

NEVER BELIEVE
THAT A FEW CARING
PEOPLE CAN'T
CHANGE THE WORLD.

Cancer friends and family

Everyone needs a Cancer friend. You are a loyal, caring, funny companion and you know how to keep a secret! Unless you have some Fire or Air in your birth chart, you can be a little shy at first when meeting new people. But when you do make a friend, you're usually buddies for life. You're the best listener and offer support where you can. Even with long-distance friendships, as soon as you get together again, you slot back like peas in a pod, as though you've never been apart.

Old friends know how to calm you down if you've been worrying or overanalysing. They're used to you dramatising your own woes and know you just need to vent your concerns. After a sympathetic ear and a few glasses of wine, you feel reassured that the world is a safe place and can let your crabby defences relax once more.

NO PLACE LIKE HOME

You're not quite happy without a hearth to call your own. Your home is your sanctuary, a safe, secure place where you come out of your shell, relax and enjoy your family. Home furnishings will be comfortable and perhaps a little weather-worn by children and pets over the years. You're sentimental about old things with personal memories attached, which can mean you end up keeping objects well after their use-by date.

Food is your comfort and your passion. A superb home cook, your family are usually spoiled by your culinary delights. Or if you're not into cooking, you'll almost certainly stuff your cupboards with quality goodies. Always finding excuses to stuff loved ones with food, when visitors come to call, there will be plenty of tasty morsels set aside for them. Wasting food is a terrible crime in your eyes, and if you can't feed it to family, friends or pets, you compost it or keep it for your wormery.

HOARDING OR BUILDING A SHELL?

You have a passion for collecting things, especially antiques or items of sentimental value. The most likely sign of the zodiac to hoard, once you have something in your home, it's difficult to let it go. Your possessions may eventually even feel like their part of your shell, a wall you build around yourself, and everything dear to you.

If you feel insecure you worry, and when you're anxious you cling to the things you love. The most prepared person for a worst-case scenario, you probably have a fully kitted out nuclear bunker or a shed full of tinned foods and bottled water. Your house is packed to the gunnels with emergency supplies, usually including out-of-date medicines, batteries and wellington boots with holes.

CANCER PARENT

Born to nurture, care and protect, you are the zodiac's most dedicated parent. You love to share your vivid imagination with your children. A wonderful storyteller and inventive game player, you understand the inner workings of your child's mind. The embodiment of tenderness and patience, you never tire of your children's demands on your time.

CANCER CHILD

Super-sensitive and prone to quick changes in mood, lunar-ruled babies often pick up on the energies around them without realising that's what they're doing. Once reassured by their parents, they feel safe and secure again, eager to learn and play. They're extremely curious but can get overwhelmed in chaotic, noisy situations. These creative little souls prefer making cakes, drawing and playing at dress-up to rough and tumble adventures.

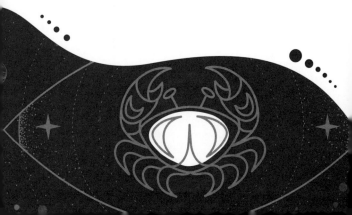

Healthy Cancer

*Y*ou're sensitive to the phases of the Moon, which push and pull your emotional states. Your fluctuating feelings are the main gauge of your wellbeing. When you're feeling happy, safe and secure, you have heaps of energy, a hearty appetite, and all feels well with the world. When your feelings are out of whack, your sensitive digestive system can be the first to feel something's not right.

Sometimes at a full Moon you need to be a little kinder to yourself, as you can be your own worst critic when you're feeling out of sorts emotionally. This state of flux can be reflected in worry or stress in your body. No other sign is as affected by their own positive or negative thoughts, and emotional states, as you. If you are prone to feeling unwell when anxious, the same should be true when you're feeling strong and therefore able to heal yourself.

FOOD AND DRINK

For better or worse, food is usually your chosen comfort. You tend to eat when you're feeling anxious, bored or excited, and sometimes just because it's delicious and wonderful! You love traditional, old restaurants steeped in history almost as much as you adore a home-cooked roast dinner with friends at home.

For you, food is best as a family affair, and you don't need much of an excuse to prepare an elaborate meal or mouth-watering cake for a birthday or special occasion.

Cooking and sampling your delicious meals can see unwanted weight creep up on you. But your talents in the kitchen means you're flexible and willing to experiment, so it shouldn't be too much of a chore to choose lighter or more unusual options.

As a Water sign, drinking plenty of fluids keeps you feeling balanced. A glass of delicious wine or an exciting cocktail will often be chosen as a special treat. If you punish yourself for eating and drinking too much, you can become entrenched in some unhealthy habits, or be subconsciously sending yourself unhelpful messages around food. 'A little bit of what you fancy does you good' would be a healthy motto.

ACTIVITIES AND RELAXATION

You dislike feeling uncomfortable, so getting sweaty and breathless isn't your thing – and aggressive forms of exercise disturbs your equilibrium. Gentler forms of physical action, such as yoga, walking, dancing and swimming, all soothe your nerves and help you coordinate your physical and emotional energies.

Being near water relaxes you almost as much as swimming in it. A walk along a beach or a stroll by a river soothes your water-ruled constitution in a magical manner. You're a sensual person and the gentle rhythm of the waves just feels right on a very primal level.

Your sense of humour also plays a vital role in keeping you upbeat. When you're laughing at life and enjoying yourself, you grab hold of it and refuse to give it up until you absolutely have to.

BODY AREA: CHEST AND BREASTS

As you are a nurturing sign it's the chest and breasts which are the areas associated with your sign. The stomach is also linked to the Crab, and because you love your food so much, you may be prone to over-indulge, causing occasional indigestion or worry-related ulcers if you're really over-anxious.

Cancer on the move

*Y*ou travel well. Your own fluctuating feelings happily mix in with the constantly changing landscape. With your family in tow, you'll usually be the person in charge of deciding where to go, when and how much it's going to cost!

As a Moon-ruled Water sign, one of the few things that will tear you away from your beloved home is the prospect of being near a beautiful watery landscape. Picnics on the banks of tranquil lakes, walks along meandering rivers or traditional seaside holidays at home, all float your boat. You prefer well-established, intimate family-friendly hotels with a personal touch rather than large, new soulless establishments. Staying in a personable bed and breakfast would be perfectly acceptable, as would a house-swap option or a cosy old pub that serves tasty home-cooked meals.

ROOTS AND RETREATS

With your love of history and fascination with your own family tree, a trip to see where your ancestors lived will be an emotionally satisfying journey. You'll experience a deep connection to the land your grandparents knew, strengthening the deep respect you have for your family roots. You also resonate with spiritual places and are one of the few zodiac signs to enjoy a meditation retreat. You value your privacy, and, for all your love of being in a family group, connecting with the 'you' beneath your shell, renews your energy and faith in life.

EMOTIONAL CURRENCY

Sensible with the pennies, you won't splurge on a holiday on impulse. You'll think it through carefully and shop around for the best deals. Staying with family or friends overseas appeals where you can catch up with loved ones while saving some hard-earned resources! The rest of your family might have a different view, but you'd probably rather book two, or more, connecting flights rather than go direct if it meant knocking a few pounds off the budget. You'll probably cater for the whole family while you're travelling too – with plenty of comfort food and tasty snacks to take the edge of the boring waits at airports or train stations.

SENTIMENTAL JOURNEY

A sentimentalist at heart, you are unlikely to be able to resist buying keepsakes and souvenirs of your trips. You're an avid collector, if not a particularly discerning one. So, if you spot any hypnotically ugly antiques or interesting hats to add to your growing collection, so be it. You also drive a surprisingly tough bargain. Local vendors and market traders are often flabbergasted at the lengths to which you'll stretch, in order to knock a few pennies off whatever you've got your beady eyes on.

Above all, it's the people you meet throughout your trips and travels that mean more to you than the places you visit. You make friends so easily because you're so curious about how other people live, and you're deeply touched if shown any kindness. You treat being invited into someone else's home as the highest honour. Take plenty of photographs as mementoes to show your family back home. Photographs are important because they help keep your memories of the past alive.

Cancer
Favourite Places

Moonlit cruise

Cosy cottage

Food festival

Your own home

Traditional seaside

Meditation retreat

Lake district

Canal boat

Cancer
BIRTHDATE
PERSONALITIES

Discover your
personal forecast
for the day of
your birth.

22 June

*Y*ou are a soft and perceptive person with an excellent memory, assets which serve you well in life. You retain information and have a shrewd mind for business. Devoted to your family and friends, you have a gift for making people feel included. You are imaginative, poetic and observant. You have an uncanny knack of being able to catch the tender and funny moments of family life with your camera or your pen. However, you are also thin-skinned and can hold onto past hurts. Learning to forgive and forget is a lifetime lesson. You value your relationships highly because you need a family of your own. Children give your life meaning. Since you are so emotional, tai chi or yoga, which strengthen the inner core, would help you to keep centred.

STRENGTHS

Strong family values, insightful

WEAKNESSES

Unforgiving and over-sensitive

MEDITATION

In time of test, family is best.

23 June

*Y*ou are a dramatic yet sensitive person with a shy exterior that hides your warm heart. You are caring and radiate such an extraordinary energy that others want to be near you. You were born to shine, are very talented with a powerful belief in yourself that comes from a happy childhood. You take the lead, whatever your gender. You are a natural performer and can be a bit of a prima donna, but people forgive you, as you truly are great at what you do. In romance you are extremely loving and attentive and give totally of yourself. You are a family person. You need a mate who is creative with a passionate nature to give you the adoration you expect. Unwind by playing games; these have immense appeal – especially those you remember from child-hood, such as skipping.

STRENGTHS

Self-confident and considerate to the needs of others

WEAKNESSES

Egotistical and needy

MEDITATION

There is no pillow so soft as a clear conscience.

24 June

*Y*ou are a delightfully imaginative person who is always kind and helpful to others. You are concerned for the well-being of people and offer practical support. You are thoughtful; a person who remembers birthdays and anniversaries. You are efficient; an asset nowadays since so many people lead busy lives. You could make a career from sorting out the mess in somebody's home or office – filing is your forté! Your clear head and natural concern for the feelings of others means you would never throw away what they might treasure. A happy and committed relationship is a priority for you, and you will work at making it last. At times you can be over-fussy and caught up in trivia. A massage is ideal for when your mind gets bogged down in the minutiae of life.

STRENGTHS
Considerate, organized

WEAKNESSES
Fussy and uptight

MEDITATION
*It's not what you look at
that matters, it's what
you see.*

25 June

*Y*ou are a gracious and likeable person with a strong need to be appreciated for your talents and beauty. You enjoy giving pleasure to people and take a genuine delight in making others happy. You have a social conscience and are patriotic, but can be overly defensive if anyone criticizes your family or your country. You enjoy being a part of a large organization and will be drawn to work in human resources. Your weakness is your tendency to indecision as you don't like to upset people. You settle into a loving relationship early and become a devoted parent. However, you also need to be adored and pampered. When you get down in the doldrums, a trip to the hairdresser will cheer you up and a new outfit will restore your self-esteem.

STRENGTHS
Charming and righteous

WEAKNESSES
Hesitant with decision making, oversensitive

MEDITATION
A wise man makes his own decisions, an ignorant man follows public opinion.

26 June

*Y*ou are a charismatic and intensely emotional person who is unforgettable. There is an air of mystery about you and you can be a master of disguise. When hurt you sulk and can retreat into your shell for a long time until your wounds are healed. You delve into your emotions and love to investigate the dark side of life. You are a superb detective and you love to be entrusted with secrets. You are attracted to a career in the police force or forensics. You are tenacious and determined and have an inner core that can survive almost anything. You need to be adored and usually have many suitors. The one you choose understands that your defences hide a soft and sensitive underbelly. A family outing with a difference such as visiting underground caves will thrill and fascinate you.

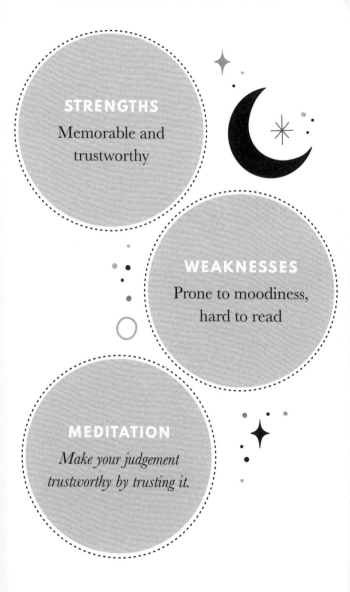

STRENGTHS
Memorable and trustworthy

WEAKNESSES
Prone to moodiness, hard to read

MEDITATION
Make your judgement trustworthy by trusting it.

27 June

*Y*ou are a colourful and dramatic person with a delicate and soothing touch that people love. You set yourself big juicy goals and dedicate yourself to fulfilling them. You have an inner faith that inspires you and others. Throughout your life you reach out to huge groups of people. There is a creative flair about everything you do, but you can be too hasty and overlook the details. In business you are the entrepreneur and need a backup team to support you. In a personal relationship you expect a lot of freedom and need someone who totally supports your endeavours. You relate well to people but have an introverted side and need private space to totally relax and recuperate. A desert island would suit you, but on a practical level going to the sauna or hot tub would be bliss.

STRENGTHS
Calming and
inspirational

WEAKNESSES
Rash and over-reliant
on others

MEDITATION
*Be prepared to live with the
consequences of a decision.*

28 June

*Y*ou are a person with an air of authority, whose strong leadership skills tend to overshadow your soft and caring centre. You are a pillar of strength in a crisis because you are solid and dependable. You are in touch with your feelings, which means you respond rather than react. You reach out to people in a maternal way, yet have the attributes of a wise father. At times you are overcontrolling and treat people as if they are children. You are a romantic and seek a relationship where your mate is also your ally. The added bonus for you would be if you could work well together at a business. A laconic sense of humour is your biggest asset. You tend to contract your chest to protect yourself. Swimming, especially breaststroke, would be tremendously beneficial for you.

STRENGTHS
Trustworthy, with a dry sense of humour

WEAKNESSES
Dominant and, at times, patronizing

MEDITATION
One never needs their humour as much as when they argue with a fool.

29 June

You are a kind-hearted person, a progessive with a strong intellect. You are deeply concerned with the family of man, and you truly believe all people are created equally. You reach out to people and gather many friends in the course of your life. You are fascinated by radical ideas and love to debate with others. However, you can cling to your friends and family and become overprotective of them. Your people skills would serve you as a politician because you are keen to be involved with the public's welfare. In love you can be attracted to a bohemian lifestyle in your youth as you value freedom, but later on your emotional need for a home and nesting takes over. Playing a game of chess or practising an unconventional sport such as hang-gliding are great ways for you to unwind.

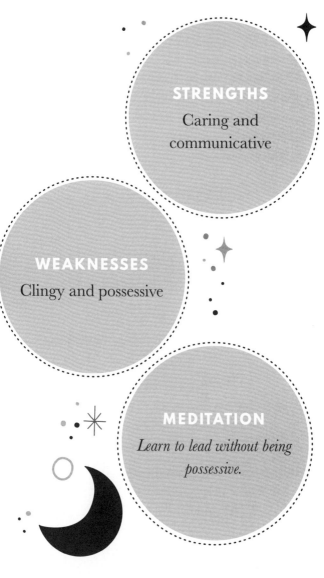

STRENGTHS
Caring and
communicative

WEAKNESSES
Clingy and possessive

MEDITATION
*Learn to lead without being
possessive.*

30 June

*Y*ou are a colourful and expressive person who hides the fact they are a sensitive soul behind a façade of wit and practical jokes. You have a wonderful gift with comedy and your jokes lift people's spirits. You move quickly and gracefully and have a friendly and bubbly manner that is enchanting. You would do well in PR because you love to talk to new people. You enjoy circulating and networking and you mix in a wide circle. You speak from your heart. However, you remember past hurts – a trait which does not serve you well. In a relationship you value someone who is gentle and tender; you need to trust a person before you open up to them completely. A daily diary where you write down what brought you happiness that day would greatly promote a positive outlook.

STRENGTHS
Eloquent and lively

WEAKNESSES
Find it hard to forgive
and forget – which
breeds negativity

MEDITATION
*The person who says
it cannot be done should not
interrupt the person
doing it.*

1 July

*Y*ou are a spontaneous and volatile person who has a strong sense of your individuality. You will fight for your rights and are also sensitive and protective of the rights of others. You have a lot to give but can be demanding and need a lot of affection and reassurance from others to feel secure. There is a certain childlike quality about you, and on occasions you can be highly temperamental if things don't go your way. You bounce back once your concerns are listened to. You can be forthright in your opinions and put your foot in your mouth when you speak before you think. Relationships fulfil you emotionally but can be a mix of tenderness and fights. A sport such as kickboxing or maybe playing table tennis with the family will allow you to release pent-up feelings in a fun way.

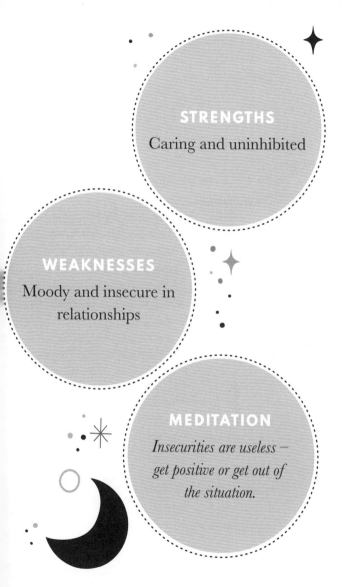

STRENGTHS

Caring and uninhibited

WEAKNESSES

Moody and insecure in relationships

MEDITATION

Insecurities are useless — get positive or get out of the situation.

2 July

*Y*ou are a caring and dependable person whose values are rooted in a love of the countryside and of nature. You have a strong artistic ability and musical talent. There is always a song in your head and you often hum softly to yourself. You are tenacious and hold onto friends, claiming them and their loyalty. You know what the public want and would do well in the restaurant or entertainment business. At work or at home you are quite happy to be second in command, rather than take the lead. Family life is your priority and you are a faithful partner. In love affairs your controlling streak can stifle your mate and ruin your relationship. You relax easily, and lethargy can take over. A daily routine of walking while listening to music will ground you and restore inner peace.

STRENGTHS
Creative and caring

WEAKNESSES
Prone to sluggishness,
possessive

MEDITATION
*Idleness is the mother of
all vices.*

3 July

*Y*ou are a person with a great variety of faces as you adapt brilliantly to whomever you are with. You can easily imitate others which is great fun for you and highly entertaining for them. You are sensitive and so can use this gift with skill and not offend anyone. NLP (Neuro-Linguistic Programing) is a perfect training and profession for you because connecting with people is what you do naturally. You are influenced by what others think of you and pick up on atmosphere, so can get unexpectedly depressed. In relationships you are quixotic which can be confusing for your partner. You care deeply one minute then are light and breezy the next. Balance is important for you to maintain; too much talking and empathizing wears you out, so escape for a while and read a good book.

STRENGTHS
Versatile and
understanding

WEAKNESSES
Unrealistic and
oversensitive

MEDITATION
*It takes courage to grow up
and become who you
really are.*

4 July

*Y*ou are an emotional and sensitive person who cares deeply about how others feel. You are governed by your feelings and are influenced, probably without realizing it, by the moon's monthly cycles. Just as it waxes and wanes so you can feel joy one day and gloom the next. If you focus your energy on helping those around you, you can change your mood when feeling down. You work well in the public sector, assisting those in need of protection. You are just the person to represent them and this is where your tenacity becomes an asset. You can marry young; having a secure and stable home life is essential to your happiness. You are a bit of a worrier, which upsets your sensitive stomach, so take care to listen to what your body needs and avoid spicy foods.

STRENGTHS

Determined and
understanding

WEAKNESSES

Anxious and prone
to depression

MEDITATION

*Fall seven times,
stand up eight.*

5 July

*Y*ou are an affectionate and devoted person who has high aspirations to fulfil your creative potential. You have an imperious, almost regal, air about you and naturally take a leadership position. You work well with both sexes as you are well balanced. You can be a little conceited at times. Your weakness reveals itself when others don't do what you say – you then cut off from them until they obey you. However, you eventually learn to laugh at yourself which helps bring people back on side; with age you should learn how to resist the urge to control. You are the star in the show and amateur dramatics will delight you if you're not a professional actor – you see life as production. In relationships you jump in heart first and love the idea of love. You respond to romantic gestures and any gift from a child melts you.

STRENGTHS
Loving and tender

WEAKNESSES
Bossy and unable to take orders from others

MEDITATION
No man is an island, entire of itself; every man is a piece of the continent.

6 July

*Y*ou are a sympathetic and loyal person with enormous integrity. You have a strong sense of duty which was instilled at an early age. You have a desire to serve and dedicate yourself to that purpose. However, you are tremendously sensitive to criticism and get hurt easily by an unkind word. The result is you become extremely self-protective and you can appear to hold yourself back. When stressed you get nervous and can find yourself mumbling. You have sound common sense and old-fashioned values with a close family to support you. Your relationship is your safe haven; a place where you receive the nurturing you deserve. You can get caught in worry and suffer from nervous complaints. A relaxing stroll in beautiful surroundings with a congenial companion is good for your well-being.

STRENGTHS

Dutiful, honest

WEAKNESSES

Anxious and restrained

MEDITATION

See each day as a blank canvas and make it a masterpiece.

7 July

You are a perceptive and kind-hearted person blessed with a fine intellect. You have original and progressive ideas. Someone who takes action, you push through your concepts with eloquence and determination. You can be a bit of an intellectual snob and struggle to mix with people of a lower intellect. You have an innate talent for beauty and harmony and are gifted at interior design as you have natural home-making skills. Feng shui or vastu would appeal to you. You are a perfectionist and complain when people aren't up to your high standards of excellence. Relationships suit you because you need someone to create a balance in your life, but they need to be your intellectual equal. Love poetry, soft romantic music and a bunch of scented flowers are the perfect gifts to give yourself and share with your beloved.

STRENGTHS
Well-read and resolute

WEAKNESSES
Elitist with impossibly high standards

MEDITATION
A book is like a garden carried in the pocket.

8 July

You are a magnetic and entrancing person. You are sensual and very attractive. You are highly subjective and respond by what you feel at the time rather than with logic. You can be fretful and it is difficult to get you out of a bad mood once you sink into one. You are perceptive and your radar for how others are feeling is superb. You do well in the fields of psychoanalysis and child welfare. You can handle death and birth so midwifery is also ideal. You have a satirical sense of humour and you love busting taboos, but this is not to everyone's tastes! Your relationship is intense and your partner needs to give constant reassurance if you are not to be irrationally jealous. When emotions take over, moving your body by cycling or walking near a river will restore you.

STRENGTHS
Bewitching and insightful

WEAKNESSES
Insecure and prone to anxiety attacks

MEDITATION
See things as you would have them be instead of as they are.

9 July

You are a good humoured, affable and utterly honest person. You have an enthusiasm and optimistic outlook on life that gets you through the darkest of times – you will always take the positive from a situation. For you, life has to have meaning, and you can be religious or spiritual. You are restless and impatient; a doer rather than a thinker, you can't abide time wasters. Your greatness comes from a combination of being in touch with people's feelings and your vision of a positive future. You can be outspoken yet charming, so people are beguiled. You are vulnerable. A close relationship is important for you. You need someone who loves to talk as much as you do and shares your philosophy. You need to let off steam so watching an exciting sport where you can cheer your heart out is excellent.

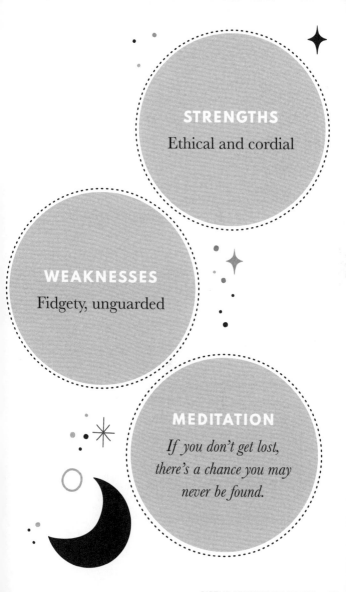

STRENGTHS
Ethical and cordial

WEAKNESSES
Fidgety, unguarded

MEDITATION
*If you don't get lost,
there's a chance you may
never be found.*

10 July

Y ou are a loyal and responsible person with good listening skills which makes you a well-liked and trusted confidant. You have old-fashioned values and love tradition. You are ambitious and work hard in life to get to the top. A true patriot, you work out of love, for your kin and your country. You have a protective instinct which is admirable. You will always keep to the letter of the law. You are shrewd at business, especially as you mature. You need to be respected. You have an air of gravitas about you and people often comment that you are too serious. The single life is not for you; you yearn for a secure and stable relationship and for someone to be waiting for you when you get home. Swimming is a perfect antidote to all the hard work you do.

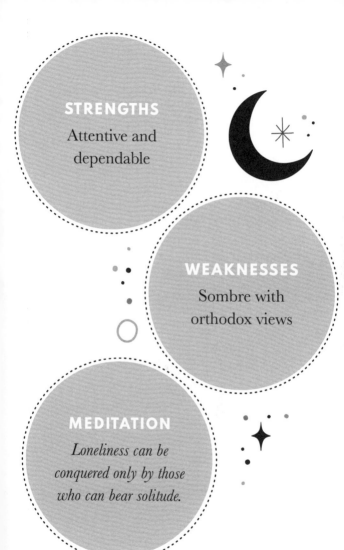

STRENGTHS
Attentive and
dependable

WEAKNESSES
Sombre with
orthodox views

MEDITATION
*Loneliness can be
conquered only by those
who can bear solitude.*

11 July

*Y*ou are a loving and compassionate person with a fine intellect. You are generous and charitable – a humanitarian who can communicate your ideas with a heartfelt conviction that encourages others to take action. You are attracted to societies and groups that support human rights. You love symbols and metaphors and learning how to decipher dreams. You are naturally gifted as an astrologer or tarot reader. Social work is also a good profession for you. You are unpredictable and change your mind depending on how you are feeling. Your weakness is that you can go into yourself to avoid emotional upsets, preferring to sort out the world's problems rather than your own. A partner who shares your convictions is essential, and with a light touch who can cajole you to lighten up when you get too heavy.

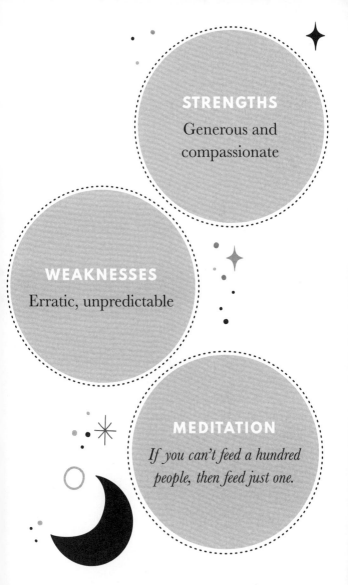

STRENGTHS
Generous and
compassionate

WEAKNESSES
Erratic, unpredictable

MEDITATION
*If you can't feed a hundred
people, then feed just one.*

12 July

*Y*ou are an imaginative person with brilliant creative gifts to give to the world. You can touch the souls of people with what you express because you are connected to the divine. At times you can feel overwhelmed by the suffering in the world and watching scenes of starvation or victims of state violence can be too much for your tender heart. Assisting humankind is second nature to you. However, you need to learn to say no to requests for help or you will fall into a pattern of sacrifice. You also need to take care of yourself emotionally and physically. You are easily misled in romance and can try and rescue people, so reflect before you commit to one person. Laughter is the best medicine for lifting your mood. A partner and friends who are grounded and practical are best for you.

STRENGTHS
Highly creative,
solicitous

WEAKNESSES
Unable to say no,
vulnerable

MEDITATION
*To grow up is to accept
vulnerability and move on.*

13 July

*Y*ou are a highly subjective person with a radar for how other people are feeling. You give compassion, affection and understanding and in return you expect the same. People feel an immediate rapport with you. However, at times you can overflow with feeling and get very needy, which can be smothering. You adore history and love acquiring valuables and antiques. You have many collections and hold onto things for sentimental reasons. This results in you being a hoarder so periodic clearouts are essential. Being the faithful type there's a strong chance you'll marry your childhood sweetheart. Your relationship gives you the stability you crave. You require an earthy and practical person to balance you. If you get caught up with negative feelings, reach out for help. You respond well to flower essences or homeopathy.

STRENGTHS
Sympathetic and
kindhearted

WEAKNESSES
Overwhelming,
a hoarder

MEDITATION
*If you never fail,
you will never succeed.*

14 July

A demonstrative and imaginative person, you inspire others by your courage and leadership. You are kind and open-hearted, and have a real gift of hospitality, always making others welcome. You are great at promoting a person or cause you believe in, and your endorsement makes a world of difference. This could be a good career choice for you as people take you seriously. You have an artistic streak and are an avid collector of fine and precious artefacts, especially gold jewellery. You know the value of things. In relationships you are an ardent lover and want to impress and dazzle your partner, but you also want to rule the roost. They will be more than satisfied basking in the glow of your love. A family barbecue with you at the helm will always be a success and please others as much as yourself.

STRENGTHS
Accommodating,
valiant

WEAKNESSES
An exhibitionist,
controlling

MEDITATION
*Don't show off every day,
or you will stop surprising
people.*

15 July

*Y*ou are a responsive and attentive person with excellent powers of observation. These qualities enable you to make pertinent and witty remarks about people and the human condition. You are gifted at writing – especially scripts for soap operas or composing a daily journal or blog. The rush of daily life can throw you off balance and you can get caught in attending to everyone's needs. You are reflective and need time alone to commune with your inner world. You are naturally dexterous, so a hobby such as knitting brings you joy as you love to create something useful. There is an essential purity about you and you thrive in a relationship where your partner is faithful and enjoys pottering around chatting with you. Asian-style cooking which involves a lot of chopping is very therapeutic.

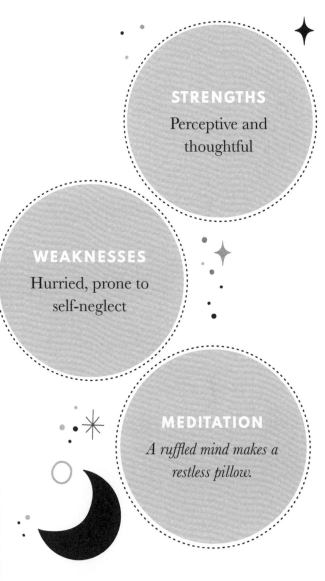

STRENGTHS
Perceptive and
thoughtful

WEAKNESSES
Hurried, prone to
self-neglect

MEDITATION
*A ruffled mind makes a
restless pillow.*

16 July

*Y*ou are a graceful and sophisticated person with immense style about all you do. You are both compassionate and caring. You have good powers of observation and have artistic gifts and refined taste. You want to be part of the fashionable set – the in-crowd – and have a powerful need to be recognized. You love being the public face of a company, so working in show business or public relations would suit you. You take pride in your image and can appear vain when in public, but can be perfectly happy in old and comfortable clothes at home. In love you are affectionate and dote on your partner, and in return they provide the security you cherish. You also need and value friends and won't put up with a possessive partner. Dancing cheek to cheek with a partner is your idea of heaven.

STRENGTHS

Elegant and tender

WEAKNESSES

Vain, self-aggrandizing

MEDITATION

No truly great person ever thought themselves so.

17 July

*Y*ou are a compelling and seductive person with natural dignity. You are attracted to danger and can be quite daring, taking big risks. People never quite know you, because you guard your private life. In turn you respect the privacy of others. You can come across as proud and haughty, but this is just your outer shell. You have a soft and sentimental side which shows itself when you are with your family. You are a born researcher and investigator and revel in a career that tests you emotionally and intellectually. You could work as a counsellor and adviser to powerful people because you can keep their secrets. Your relationships are complex; anything straightforward bores you. Once committed, you are in for the long term. A murder-mystery play or movie is a real treat for you.

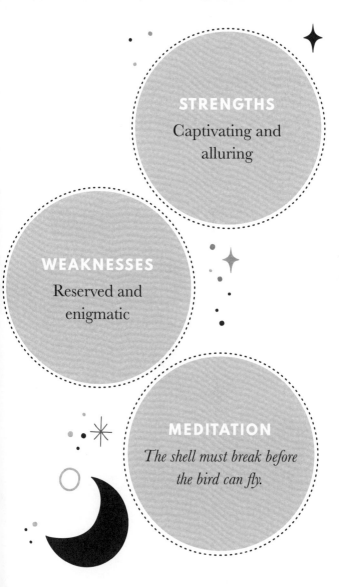

STRENGTHS
Captivating and
alluring

WEAKNESSES
Reserved and
enigmatic

MEDITATION
*The shell must break before
the bird can fly.*

18 July

You are an expansive and generous person with strong moral integrity. You have two aspects to you. Your public persona is open and good humoured but in private you are shy and sensitive. You seek justice for others and can talk convincingly about a pet cause. You are drawn towards a career as a charity worker or as an explorer. You are a born romantic and adore symphonic music and operas that sweep you away. You thrive in a personal relationship. You enjoy making expensive gestures – a weekend away with your partner somewhere lavish is typical. You are prone to mood swings because you have such high expectations about people and get crushed if they don't live up to your ideal. Hiking and camping are activities that suit your style – you live for adventure.

STRENGTHS
Loving, fair

WEAKNESSES
Temperamental,
over idealistic

MEDITATION
*Make sure you have more
than just ideals.*

19 July

*Y*ou are a considerate person who is very self-aware. Work is important to you and you are professional through and through. Everything you do is planned to last for the long term. You are self-reflective and understanding of your own – and other people's – emotions. Training is a priority for you. You could become a family therapist or work in a children's home. Although you are well-mannered, you are no pushover and can stand your ground with an authority way beyond your years. In a relationship you need time to decide if they are 'the one' and won't be forced into making a hasty decision. They, in turn, feel you are being elusive. When upset you can close down and sulk for days. Rowing is an excellent exercise for you in that it strengthens you physically and, being on water, soothes you emotionally.

STRENGTHS
Assertive and mindful

WEAKNESSES
Evasive, prone to moodiness

MEDITATION
Even if happiness forgets you a little bit, never completely forget about it.

20 July

*Y*ou are a down-to-earth, sensual person with a deep connection to the place where you were born. You have luxurious tastes and appreciate things that are tactile and beautiful to look at. Good design matters to you and you are able to make a career out of it. You are kind and helpful in what you say and do, and always offer practical advice. You are a capable organizer and take a methodical approach to tasks. A long-term relationship gives you the stability you seek, and you love taking care of your family. You love to be cosy and are content to stay at home with your beloved. Nevertheless, you can be stubborn and get irritable when tired, or if you haven't eaten for a while. Watch your blood sugar levels and carry a snack with you to keep your energy levels up.

STRENGTHS

Kindhearted, pragmatic

WEAKNESSES

Obstinate and tetchy

MEDITATION

Remember to eat — the belly rules the mind.

21 July

*Y*ou are a witty and kind-hearted person who has a gift of empathy; you truly understand what it is to walk in someone else's shoes. This uncanny knack of identifying with other people's emotions makes you a natural counsellor. Even if this isn't your chosen profession people feel comfortable pouring their hearts out to you. This can be tiring because you have the tendency to neglect yourself while you take on everyone else's problems. You need some time to yourself in order to unwind – and a confidant of your own to share what's going on in your life. Relationships are essential as you are always communicating. You need a partner who is fun-loving because you can be quite childish at times. Keeping a daily journal is an excellent way to contact your inner world.

STRENGTHS

Entertaining and understanding

WEAKNESSES

Manic and immature

MEDITATION

Maturity is knowing when to be immature.

22 July

*Y*ou are a nurturing and motherly person who is incredibly receptive to the emotions of others around you. It is as if you have no skin and can be prone to catch any bug that is going around. Early in life you have to acquire a protective shell or you would not survive. Everyone turns to you for help and you can end up taking care of every waif and stray in the neighbourhood. By getting too absorbed with others you sometimes neglect your own considerable talents as a writer or musician. You tend to live close to your birth place, but water is your element, so you're happiest living by the sea or a river. An intimate relationship supports your growth and allows you to blossom. You can stagnate, so a detox would be an effective way to clear you energetically.

STRENGTHS

Protective,
open-minded

WEAKNESSES

Sluggish, prone to
self-neglect

MEDITATION

*Bad habits are easier
to abandon today than
tomorrow.*

Going
DEEPER

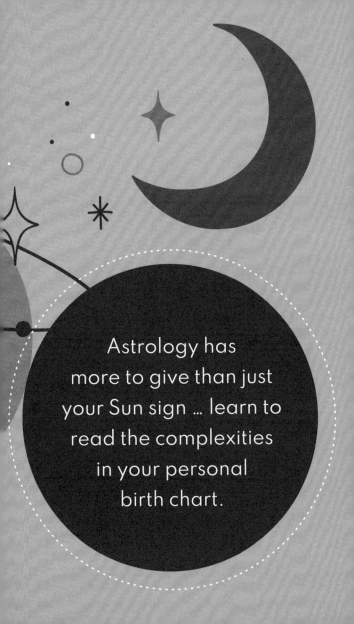

Astrology has more to give than just your Sun sign ... learn to read the complexities in your personal birth chart.

Your personal birth chart

*U*nderstanding your Sun sign is an essential part of astrology, but it's the tip of the iceberg. To take your astrological wisdom to the next level, you'll need a copy of your unique birth chart – a map of the heavens for the precise moment you were born. You can find your birth chart at the Free Horoscopes link at: www.astro.com.

ASTROLOGICAL SYNTHESIS

When you first explore your chart, you'll find that as well as a Sun sign, you also have a Moon sign, plus a Mercury, Venus, Mars, Jupiter, Saturn, Neptune, Uranus and Pluto sign – and that they all mean something different. Then there's astrological houses to consider, ruling planets and Rising signs, aspects and element types – all of which you will learn more about in the birth chart section on pages 112–115.

The art to astrology is in synthesising all this intriguing information to paint a picture of someone's character, layer by layer. Now that you understand your Cancer Sun personality better, it's time to go deeper, and to look at the next layer – your Moon sign. To find your own Moon sign go to pages 104–111.

THE MOON'S INFLUENCE

After the Sun, your Moon sign is the second biggest astrological influence in your birth chart. It describes your emotional nature – your feelings, instincts and moods and how you respond to different sorts of people and situations. By blending your outer, Cancer Sun character with your inner, emotional, Moon sign, you'll get a much more balanced picture. If you don't feel that you're 100% Cancer, your Moon sign will probably explain why!

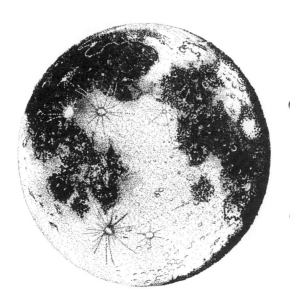

Cancer with Moon signs

CANCER SUN/**ARIES MOON**

Your Aries Moon is much quicker to react than your shyer Cancer Sun, and your emotions are nearer the surface. You're a kind, passionate soul, and when you're provoked you can sometimes say things in anger, that you later regret. This combination could give you a slightly see-sawing personality, where on the one hand you want to take immediate action, and on the other you can be quite cautious. When you do decide to go for something, you're quite gung-ho and you're less offended by criticism than a through-and-through Cancer. You are very protective of the people you love, and everybody wants you on their side because they know you can be a formidable enemy!

CANCER SUN/**TAURUS MOON**

Your Cancer tenacity combined with your solid, Taurus determination gives you an unshakeable, dependable, sense of purpose. You work slowly and, at times, indirectly towards your goals, often fooling others into thinking you'll never get there. But you always do. Usually good with money, your Taurus/

Cancer blend appreciates how to save, and you look after your investments wisely. You don't blow your own trumpet as often as you should – you're not flashy, brash or arrogant, but you have the talent and emotional maturity to easily outshine the competition. You can be something of a closed book, choosing only to share your deeper feelings with a select few. But you are loyal to the core and never forget another's kindness.

CANCER SUN/**GEMINI MOON**

Less emotionally attached than most Cancer Suns, you're open, friendly and inquisitive. Your feelings are as tuned-in to your immediate surroundings as your thoughts are and you know instinctively when someone is not telling you the whole truth. Your warmth and affection attracts many friends and you care for everyone who needs it, including pigeons and stray dogs! You're quite experimental in your relationships and give your partner plenty of freedom. But if you're not shown respect in return you may retreat into your hard shell. Your changeable Gemini moods may take over if you're feeling unsure of yourself but you're generally a trusting, sentimental person with a huge appetite for fun.

CANCER SUN/**CANCER MOON**

You're a new Moon baby – born when both the Sun and Moon were passing through the same sign of the zodiac. This doubling of the zodiac energies involved strengthens the personality traits of the sign. Intuitive to a fault, your impressions of others borders on psychic. You're a deeply sensitive and caring person. When somebody you care about says or does something thoughtless, you can take it quite personally. That other people don't always mean what they say is probably one of the hardest lessons that you've had to learn. When you're challenged or feel threatened, you can come across as a really tough cookie. You retreat into your shell and can appear quite aggressive, but you're only protecting your soft-hearted, loving and quite vulnerable heart. It takes time for you to trust people, but when you do decide to take off your armour, they meet a deeply kind and generous person.

CANCER SUN/**LEO MOON**

As a Leo Moon person, you're proud and creative and you care what people think of you and are keen to make a good impression. You're passionate and disciplined and sensitive to others' ideas and feelings. Fiercely protective over the people you love, you can be hot-headed and brave and stand up for yourself in an argument. You like to entertain people – especially at home – and your generous dinner parties are probably legendary. You have a flair for the dramatic and may have a flamboyant dress sense. Only the best is good enough for your nearest and dearest and you're not scared to spend money on quality goods. Your lavish tastes and grand gestures can take their toll on your bank account, and curbing your spending feels anathema. You show your love by treating people and expect some of that attention to come back your way.

CANCER SUN/**VIRGO MOON**

Wise, measured and practical, you don't rush into making hard and fast judgments about people. You're a planner and organiser, and you're excellent at remembering the little important details about other people, which makes them feel special. You're probably a thoughtful gift-buyer too, never leaving Christmas or birthday presents to the last minute. Sometimes a little impatient, you're keen to show others how to improve, and you'll need to discover a way of approaching this tactfully as it could be interpreted as criticism. You have an excess of nervous emotional energy, which can show itself in unnecessary worry or you might just find it hard to stay still. As a Virgo Moon, chaos and emotional turmoil can play havoc with your nerves. You need a healthy routine to keep you feeling optimistic and in control.

CANCER SUN/**LIBRA MOON**

You strive to keep the peace in all your relationships. Confrontation alarms you and you'll avoid it where you can. You believe there's a happy compromise to any challenging situation and are deft at weighing the pros and cons. You're not a demeaning person and have a large circle of friends and supporters. Upset by ugliness or rudeness, you prefer refined, clever people and usually desire those qualities in any potential partners. Amorous and soft, you're won over by romantic gestures, poetry and gentle, calm surroundings. You are charming and even-tempered, rarely raising your voice. But if pushed too far you'll use some carefully chosen words that will cut to the core. Libra/Cancer may be charm personified, but you'll not be taken advantage of!

CANCER SUN/**SCORPIO MOON**

Scorpio is a deep but silent Water sign which blends easily with your own Water-based Sun sign. You are one of the most emotionally strong people in the zodiac and you don't react to petty annoyances. It has to be something pretty big to upset your Scorpio Moon, but if you are pushed too far, your cutting remarks can be devastating. It can take you a long time to truly trust and care for new people in your life and you don't take your heart lightly. Nobody takes a Cancer/Moon person for granted and if someone hurts you, you'll not shout, stamp your feet or show any outwards signs of emotion. You will just cut the person who broke your trust out of your life forever.

CANCER SUN/**SAGITTARIUS MOON**

 Your freedom-loving, extroverted devil-may-care Sagittarius Moon is a little at odds with your cautious, shyer Cancer Sun. Your Sagittarian emotional response is usually to jump in at the deep end, and to cross any bridges when you come to them. But your Cancer Sun is not so sure. You will have probably gone through your fair share of trial and error when it comes to romance. Sagittarius likes to experience life at every level, and you have probably bounded into a few relationships without much forethought – and bounced right back out again! Your blunt, open, Sagittarius Moon demands honesty, and your sensitive Cancer side will quickly detect if your other half is being insincere. You can get very defensive if you suspect something is amiss but your frank discourse with those you care about, usually creates an easy and honest flow of communication.

CANCER SUN/**CAPRICORN MOON**

 Capricorn is your opposite sign of the zodiac, showing you were born at a full Moon. The Moon and Sun reflect what each sign can learn from each other, and with a Goat Moon, you recognise that your comfort zone – the security of home and family life – is not all there is to life. Your lesson is to find the balance between achieving a nurturing, caring environment and being respected for your talents in the outside world. People often underestimate you, for under that charming, soft-spoken and beautifully mannered outer shell is a quietly ambitious, shrewd and disciplined person. You are a stoic, working calmly and surely to get your heart's desire – quietly working around any obstacles until you have what you want. Once you have what you want in your claws, you are not afraid to fight to keep it.

CANCER SUN/**AQUARIUS MOON**

Aquarius Moons are quite detached and logical, which will probably ground your emotionally reactive Sun. You are an extremely observant person, curious about all facets of human nature. Idealistic and humanitarian, one of your greatest desires is to make the world a better place. You may have some trust issues with authority or veer off the traditional path, but that's one of the many things that will make you such an intriguing friend or lover. Controlling relationships turn you off – you must have someone in your life who gives you the space and emotional freedom to be as off-centre as you like. And your Cancer Sun will defend your right to be exactly who you are.

CANCER SUN/**PISCES MOON**

You're artistic, impressionable and often live in your own imagination. With Water as your Sun and Moon sign, you feel situations first. Your instincts are astonishing, and before you have worked out what you think about something or how to act, you'll just 'know' on another level what's going on. Mentally receptive and empathic, you are tactful and gentle in your relationships. A little unrealistic romantically, you may fall for people who are unavailable or unreachable on some level or fall for people who are troubled or living a chaotic life. You think nothing of sacrificing your own needs for those of your family and loved ones, but it would be wise if you could cultivate a more independent stance. After all, you need to look after yourself before you can help anyone else.

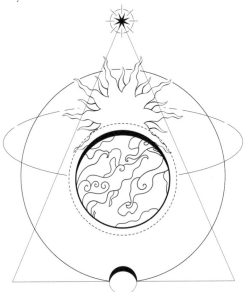

Birth charts

L earning about your Sun and Moon sign opens the gateway into exploring your own birth chart. This snapshot of the skies at the moment of birth is as complex and interesting as the person it represents. Astrologers the world over have been studying their own birth charts and those of people they know, their whole lives and still find something new in them every day. There are many schools of astrology and an inexhaustible list of tools and techniques, but here are the essentials to get you started ...

ZODIAC SIGNS AND PLANETS

These are the keywords for the 12 zodiac signs and the planets associated with them, known as ruling planets.

 ARIES
courageous, bold, aggressive, leading, impulsive

Ruling planet
 MARS
shows where you take action and how you channel your energy

TAURUS
reliable, artistic, practical, stubborn, patient

Ruling planet
VENUS
describes what you value and who and what you love

GEMINI
clever, friendly, superficial, versatile

Ruling planet
MERCURY
represents how your mind works and how you communicate

CANCER
emotional, nurturing, defensive, sensitive

Ruling planet
MOON
describes your emotional needs and how you wish to be nurtured

LEO
confidence, radiant, proud, vain, generous

Ruling planet
SUN
your core personality and character

VIRGO
analytical, organised, meticulous, thrifty

Ruling planet
MERCURY
co-ruler of Gemini and Virgo

LIBRA
fair, indecisive, cooperative, diplomatic

Ruling planet
VENUS
co-ruler of Taurus and Libra

SCORPIO
regenerating, magnetic, obsessive, penetrating

Ruling planet
PLUTO
deep transformation, endings and beginnings

SAGITTARIUS
optimistic, visionary, expansive, blunt, generous

Ruling planet
JUPITER
travel, education and faith in a higher power

CAPRICORN
ambitious, responsible, cautious, conventional

Ruling planet
SATURN
your ambitions, work ethic and restrictions

AQUARIUS
unconventional, independent, erratic, unpredictable

Ruling planet
URANUS
where you rebel or innovate

PISCES
dreamy, chaotic, compassionate, imaginative, idealistic

Ruling planet
NEPTUNE
your unconscious, and where you let things go

The 12 houses

irth charts are divided into 12 sections, known as houses, each relating to different areas of life as follows:

FIRST HOUSE

associated with *Aries*

Identity - how you appear to others and your initial response to challenges

SECOND HOUSE

associated with *Taurus*

How you make and spend money, your talents, skills and how you value yourself

THIRD HOUSE

associated with *Gemini*

Siblings, neighbours, communication and short distance travel

FOURTH HOUSE

associated with *Cancer*

Home, family, your mother, roots and the past

FIFTH HOUSE

associated with *Leo*

Love affairs, romance, creativity, gambling and children

SIXTH HOUSE

6

associated with *Virgo*

Health, routines, organisation and pets

EIGHTH HOUSE

8

associated with *Scorpio*

Sex, death, transformation, wills and money you share with another

SEVENTH HOUSE

7

associated with *Libra*

Relationships, partnerships, others and enemies

NINTH HOUSE

9

associated with *Sagittarius*

Travel, education, religious beliefs, faith and generosity

TENTH HOUSE

10

associated with *Capricorn*

Career, father, ambitions, worldly success

ELEVENTH HOUSE

11

associated with *Aquarius*

Friends, groups, ideals and social or political movements

TWELFTH HOUSE

12

associated with *Pisces*

Spirituality, the unconscious mind, dreams and karma

THE ELEMENTS

Each zodiac sign belongs to one of the four elements – Earth, Air, Fire and Water – and these share similar characteristics, as listed below.

EARTH

Taurus, Virgo, Capricorn

Earth signs are practical, trustworthy, thorough and logical.

AIR

Gemini, Libra, Aquarius

Air signs are clever, flighty, intellectual and charming.

FIRE

Aries, Leo, Sagittarius

Fire signs are active, creative, warm, spontaneous, innovators.

WATER

Cancer, Scorpio, Pisces

Water signs are sensitive, empathic, dramatic and caring.

PLANETARY ASPECTS

The aspects are geometric patterns formed by the planets and represent different types of energy. They are usually shown in two ways – in a separate grid or aspect grid and as the criss-crossing lines on the chart itself. There are oodles of different aspect patterns but to keep things simple we'll just be working with four: conjunctions, squares, oppositions and trines.

CONJUNCTION

0 degrees apart
intensifying

SQUARE

90 degrees apart
challenging

OPPOSITION

180 degrees apart
polarising

TRINE

120 degrees apart
harmonising

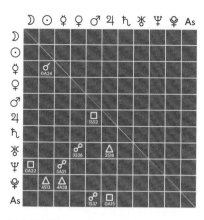

Planetary aspects for Leyla's chart

HOUSES AND RISING SIGN

Each chart is a 360° circle, divided into 12 segments known as the houses (see pages 116–117 for house interpretations). The most important point in a birth chart is known as the Rising sign, also known as the Ascendant. This is usually shown as ASC or AS on the chart and it shows the zodiac sign that was rising on the Eastern horizon for the moment you were born. It's always on the middle left of the chart on the dividing line of the first house – the house associated with the self, how you appear to others, and the lens through which you view the world. The Rising sign is the position from where the other houses and zodiac signs are drawn in a counter-clockwise direction.

CHART RULER: The planetary ruler of a person's Rising zodiac sign is always a key player in unlocking a birth chart and obtaining a deeper understanding of it.

A SIMPLE BIRTH CHART INTERPRETATION FOR A CANCER SUN PERSON

BIRTH CHART FOR LEYLA BORN 3 JULY 1987 IN NEWCASTLE, UK AT 10.40PM

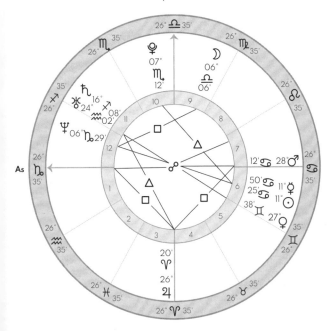

THE POSITION OF THE PLANETS: You can see that Leyla's Sun is in Cancer along with Mercury and Mars. She has Capricorn Rising, the Moon in Libra, Venus in Gemini, Jupiter in Aries, Saturn and Uranus occupy Sagittarius, Neptune's in Capricorn and Pluto sits in Scorpio.

INTERPRETATION BASICS

As well as the planetary positions, do note the houses the planets are in. How do you begin to put all these signs and symbols together? It's usually best to begin with the Sun, Rising sign and chart ruler, then look at the Moon sign.

SUN, MOON, RISING SIGN AND CHART RULER: Leyla's Sun – her outer, core personality is Cancer in the sixth house (health/work/organisation). This means she's likely to be an imaginative, caring and empathic person who expresses herself through her work. The Sun in the sixth house often indicates someone who enjoys turning a chaotic situation into something that works for everyone – she'd be a brilliant project manager.

Leyla's Libra (balance/relationships) Moon (emotions) in the ninth house (philosophy/travel) is indicative of a person who values her relationships but who needs independence and the freedom to explore (ninth house is associated with Sagittarius).

Her Rising sign is Capricorn, which describes how she approaches new situations. When people first meet someone new, they often encounter that person's Rising sign before getting to know who they really are (Sun) and then what they're like on the inside (Moon). Capricorn Rising describes a serious, determined approach to life. Her demeanour is probably quite thoughtful and considered. Saturn is Leyla's chart ruler, as it's the ruler of Capricorn. Her Saturn sits in the eleventh house of friends and groups of people, so we can assume this area of life holds special significance for her.

OTHER PLANETS: Mercury, the planet of communication, occupies Cancer in the sixth house of health and work. Leyla probably understands on an intuitive level how other people are feeling and wishes to be of practical use or service (sixth house). Venus (love/money) sits in Gemini – and is also in the sixth house (work/ organisation/daily routines). Venus's position can also describe where one might meet a potential partner – so in Leyla's case this could happen in the workplace or as part of her daily routine. Mars (action/willpower/ passion) sits in Cancer (care/intuition/moods) in the seventh house of relationships, showing she has heaps of energy for her closest relationships.

Jupiter (luck/expansion/travel) was in Aries at the time of Leyla's birth, suggesting an independent, enthusiastic zest for life and passion for adventure. As all this action happens in her third house of communication, so it looks like Leyla will have big ideas that she needs to express.

Saturn and Uranus sit together in Sagittarius in the eleventh house of groups and organisations and it's also the house that Uranus rules (associated with Aquarius). The eleventh house is also known as the house of hopes and wishes – and with Saturn's slow determination and Uranus's brilliance sitting here, Leyla will probably have the willpower and vision to create her own destiny.

Neptune (imagination) occupies the house that it rules, too, the twelfth (subconscious/dreams). This shows Leyla has a vivid imagination.

ADDING IN THE PLANETARY ASPECTS

Let's take a brief look at the strongest aspects – the ones with the most exact angles or 'orbs' to the planetary degrees (the numbers next to the planets).

MOON SQUARE NEPTUNE: Leyla is a sensitive soul (Neptune), who may sometimes find it challenging (square) to get to grip with her emotions (Moon).

SUN CONJUNCT MERCURY AND TRINE PLUTO: Leyla's ego (Sun) is strengthened (conjunction) by her intellect (Mercury) and she can use her (Pluto) insight to her advantage (trine).

MERCURY OPPOSES NEPTUNE AND TRINE PLUTO: Sometimes Leyla's ideas (Mercury) can be hard to fathom or pin down (Neptune) but her positivity (trine) and insight (Pluto) make her determined to try!

VENUS OPPOSES URANUS: Venus (love/balance/relationships) opposes (polarising) Uranus (sudden change/erratic behaviour). Leyla's closest relationships probably require change to keep them fresh and lively.

MARS SQUARE JUPITER AND OPPOSES AS (RISING SIGN): Mars (action) square (challenging) Jupiter (expansion/freedom) is a tricky aspect in Leyla's chart showing that Leyla might be prone to make hasty judgments without considering things through. Mars opposing her AS (Rising sign) indicates a feisty quality in her dealing with others.

JUPITER TRINE URANUS AND SQUARE SATURN: Leyla is lucky (Jupiter) that the changes (Uranus) in her life are usually favourable (trine). But to make the best use of these planetary energies she has to master her dislike (square) of restriction and discipline (Saturn).

YOUR JOB AS AN ASTROLOGER

The interpretation above is simplified to help you understand some of the nuts and bolts of interpretation.

Remember when you're putting the whole thing together that astrology doesn't show negatives or positives. The planets represent potential and opportunities, rather than definitions set in stone. It's your job as an astrologer to use the planets' wisdom to blend and synthesise those energies to create the picture of a whole person. It can take years to master the art of astrology but, with these simple tools as your starting point, you'll discover it is an enlightening and fascinating process!

Going deeper

To see your own birth chart visit: www.astro.com and click the Free Horoscopes link and then enter your birth information. If you don't know what time you were born, put in 12.00pm. Your Rising sign and the houses might not be right, but the planets will be in the correct zodiac signs and the aspects will be accurate.

Further reading and credits

WWW.ASTRO.COM

This amazing astrological resource is extremely popular with both experienced and beginner astrologers. It's free to sign up and obtain your birth chart and personalised daily horoscopes.

BOOKS

PARKER'S ASTROLOGY by Derek and Julia Parker (Dorling Kindersley)

THE LITTLE BOOK OF ASTROLOGY by Marion Williamson (Summersdale)

THE BIRTHDAY ORACLE by Pam Carruthers (Arcturus)

THE 12 HOUSES by Howard Sasportas (London School of Astrology)

THE ARKANA DICTIONARY OF ASTROLOGY by Fred Gettings (Penguin)

THE ROUND ART by AJ Mann (Paper Tiger)

THE LUMINARIES by Liz Greene (Weiser)

SUN SIGNS by Linda Goodman (Pan Macmillan)

Marion Williamson is a best-selling astrology author and editor. *The Little Book of Astrology* and *The Little Book of the Zodiac* (Summersdale 2018) consistently feature in Amazon's top 20 astrology books. These were written to encourage beginners to move past Sun signs and delve into what can be a lifetime's study. Marion has been writing about different areas of self-discovery for over 30 years. A former editor of *Prediction* magazine for ten years, Marion had astrology columns in *TVTimes*, *TVEasy*, *Practical Parenting*, *Essentials* and *Anglers Mail* for over ten years. Twitter: @_I_am_astrology

Pam Carruthers is a qualified professional Vedic and Western astrologer and student of *A Course in Miracles*. An experienced Life Coach and Trainer, Pam helps clients discover the hidden patterns that are holding them back in their lives. A consultation with her is a life enhancing and healing experience. She facilitates a unique transformational workshop 'Healing your Birth Story' based on your birthchart. Based in the UK, Pam has an international clientele.

All images courtesy of Shutterstock and Freepik/Flaticon.com.